MACHINES
AS TALL AS
GIANTS

PAUL STICKLAND

Random House 🏠 New York

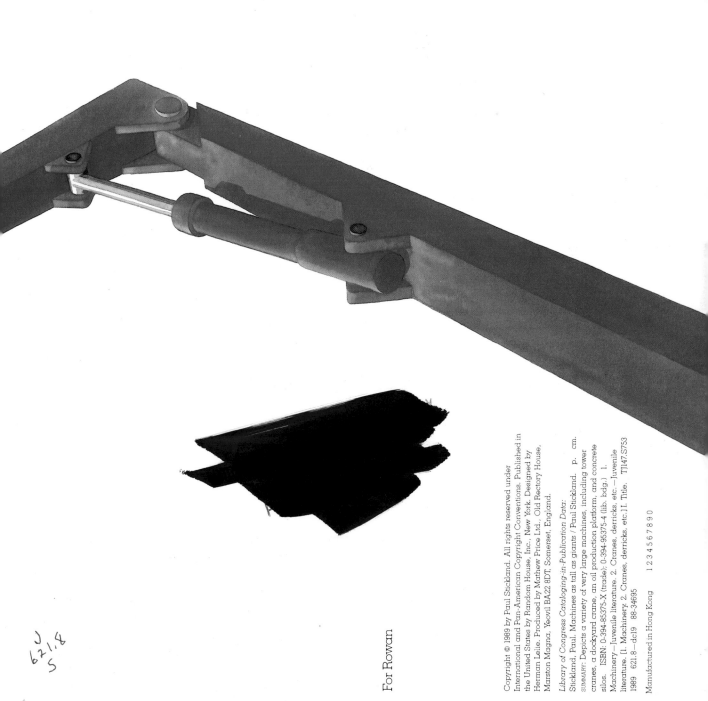

For Rowan

Copyright © 1989 by Paul Stickland. All rights reserved under
International and Pan-American Copyright Conventions. Published in
the United States by Random House, Inc., New York. Designed by
Herman Lelie. Produced by Mathew Price Ltd., Old Rectory House,
Marston Magna, Yeovil BA22 8DT, Somerset, England.

Library of Congress Cataloging-in-Publication Data:
Stickland, Paul. Machines as tall as giants / Paul Stickland.   p.   cm.
SUMMARY: Depicts a variety of very large machines, including tower
cranes, a dockyard crane, an oil production platform, and concrete
silos.   ISBN: 0-394-85375-X (trade); 0-394-95375-4 (lib. bdg.)   1.
Machinery—Juvenile literature. 2. Cranes, derricks, etc.—Juvenile
literature. [1. Machinery. 2. Cranes, derricks, etc.]1. Title.   TJ147.S753
1989   621.8—dc19   88-34695

Manufactured in Hong Kong   1 2 3 4 5 6 7 8 9 0

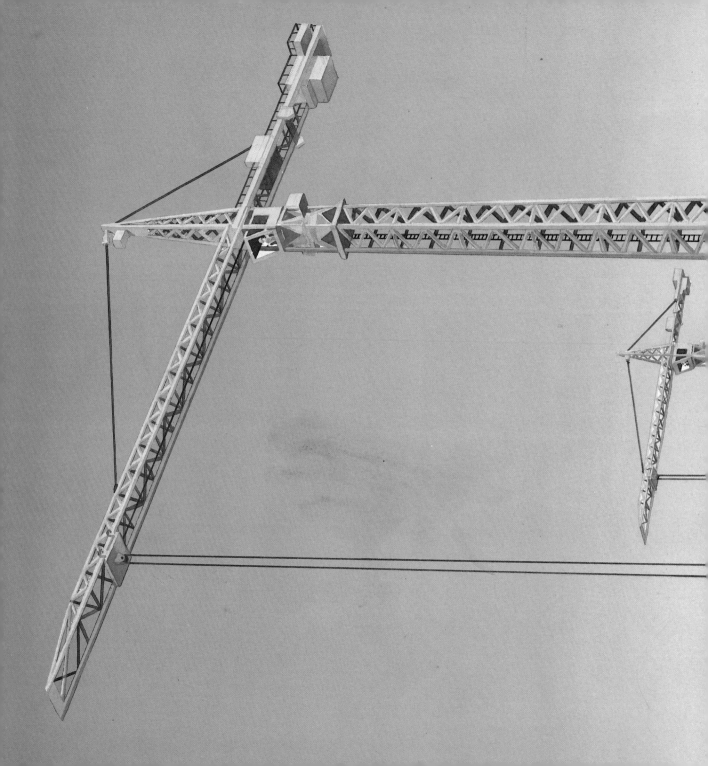

These two tower cranes were brought to the building site in parts and assembled there. The crane in the foreground is so high that the person on the ladder must climb 200 rungs to reach the top.

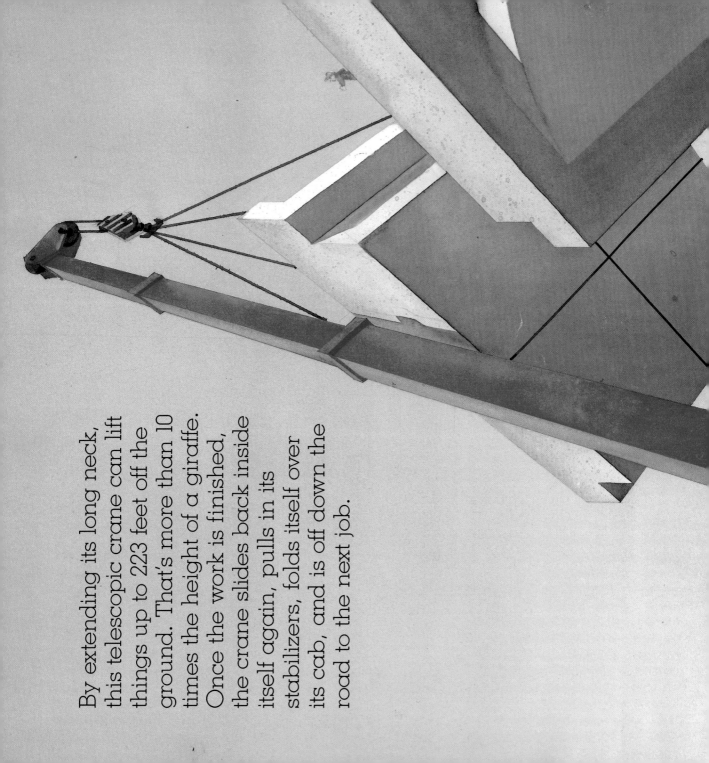

By extending its long neck, this telescopic crane can lift things up to 223 feet off the ground. That's more than 10 times the height of a giraffe. Once the work is finished, the crane slides back inside itself again, pulls in its stabilizers, folds itself over its cab, and is off down the road to the next job.

This space shuttle is as tall as an 18-story building and needs two booster rockets and an enormous fuel tank to lift it into space. Minutes later, after the shuttle is launched, the rockets and fuel tank are jettisoned. In a trip of seven days the shuttle would be able to circle the earth 112 times.

This smelting machine is an enormous furnace that makes steel for bridges and ships. When metal is heated, it glows red hot. If you heat it more, it turns white hot and melts. The very large ladle is pouring molten metal into this furnace, which can hold liquid metal weighing as much as 33 buses.

This huge machine is used to load and unload grain. It moves close to a ship and, like a gigantic vacuum cleaner, sucks the grain up its large pipes. Then the pipes are used to blow the grain into a nearby granary or fill up smaller ships alongside the dock. In one day each pipe can suck up enough grain to fill five Olympic-size swimming pools.

Fifty people would have to stand on each other's shoulders to reach the top of this cargo ship that is being worked on in a dry dock. It is made of steel plates that are riveted onto the framework and then welded until they are watertight. When the ship is finished, water will be let into the dock to make it float.

This oil production platform stands 689 feet above the ocean floor, or as tall as a 70-story building. A hole is drilled deep beneath the seabed and oil is made to flow up to the top of the platform, like water out of a giant tap.

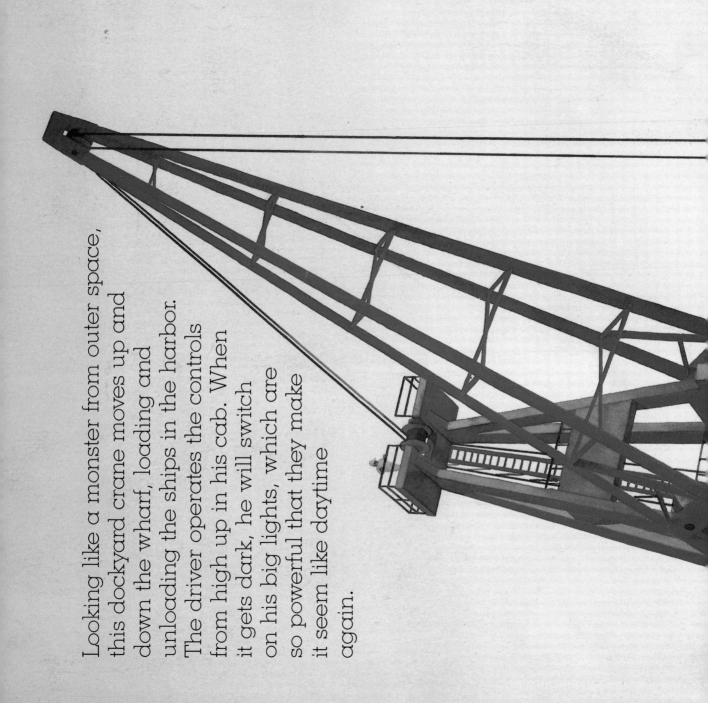

Looking like a monster from outer space, this dockyard crane moves up and down the wharf, loading and unloading the ships in the harbor. The driver operates the controls from high up in his cab. When it gets dark, he will switch on his big lights, which are so powerful that they make it seem like daytime again.

Concrete silos make liquid concrete. Mobile concrete mixers line up underneath to have their empty drums filled. One silo can fill 30 mixers. On the way to the building site the drums spin around and around so that the concrete inside them becomes thoroughly mixed and has no chance to harden before it is needed.

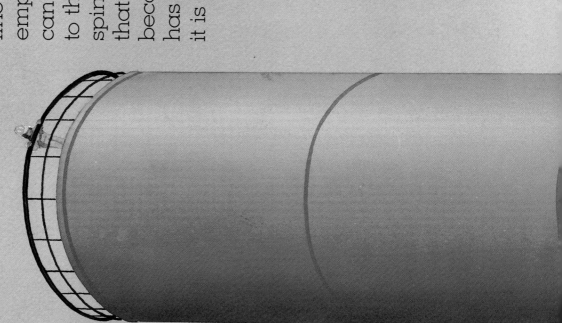

A car that has been badly damaged in an accident, or one that is very old, is taken to the car dump where this 22-wheeled car crusher gets to work on it. A large grab picks up the car and puts it into powerful jaws that close in, squashing the car into a compact cube as small as it will go.

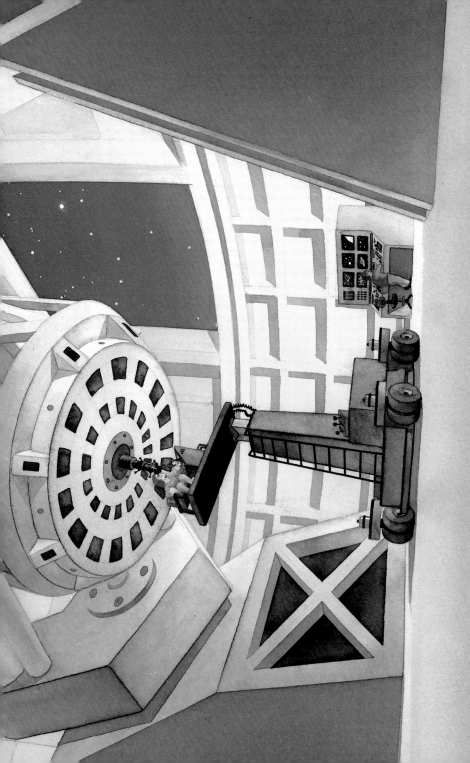

This giant telescope is as heavy as 60 buses and as high as a great oak tree. The telescope is so tall that the astronomer must sit in a hydraulic chair to reach it. When the astronomer wants to use the telescope to search for new stars and distant planets, the huge roof slides open.

The building was burning fiercely. This special fire engine, which can reach up to the 10th floor, arrived. In less than three minutes the truck's stabilizing legs were put down, its long arm put up, and the whole family was safe on its platform.